JUST BE...

Paperback ISBN 978-1-964012-57-5

Hardback ISBN 978-1-964012-58-2

There will be times when things get hard and you feel lonely. Learn to be like a sea turtle – swim alone and find comfort in being yourself. It is in those moments you will find your true meaning.

There will be times when people make you feel less than you are. Learn to be like the caterpillar – through the struggle, you will become a beautiful being with a unique story to tell. It is through those moments you will realize that the struggle is worth it, no matter how hard it may be.

There will be times when you don't know what to do. Be like a sponge – soak up all the knowledge you can. There will be people around who are happy to help and share their wisdom. Asking for help is NOT a weakness. It is a STRENGTH!

There will be times when you feel like you don't belong. Be like a tree – grow where you are. Being in one place now does not mean you will stay there forever. There is a big world to explore. Grow from your roots. You'll learn so much that one day you'll be able to go and do whatever you desire. The world is yours to take and conquer!

There will be times when you feel lost, unsure of which turn to take. Be like the ocean, a stream or a waterfall. Just go with the flow. Stay calm, enjoy the journey, and flush away negative thoughts.

There will be times when you feel confused and not sure what to do. You may feel like you don't know which direction to take or how to proceed. Be like a feather – move around without resistance.

There will be times when you are not treated fairly. People will hurt your feelings just to make you feel bad. Be like a pineapple – tough on the outside but sweet on the inside. Never let someone's negativity take away the sweetness within you.

There will be times when you feel knocked down, as if no one understands. Be like a rainbow – come out shining bright after the storm.

There will be times when you feel sad, unhappy, mad or gloomy. Don't let those days bring you down. Be like the sun – shine as bright as you are!

There will be days when people try to hold you back from your dreams and goals. Follow your own path to success. Don't let anyone stand in your way – this is your journey to your destination!

There will be days when you know exactly what you want. Be like a runner – run directly toward your dreams and goals. Don't let anyone stand in your way. Your dreams are there to guide you.

Remember this:

Just Be You!

You are Amazing and Perfect!

There is only ONE YOU!

THAT IS WHY YOU ARE UNIQUE!